AF481158

THE ALLIED POWERS VS. THE CENTRAL POWERS OF WORLD WAR I

History 6th Grade
Children's Military Books

Speedy Publishing LLC

40 E. Main St. #1156

Newark, DE 19711

www.speedypublishing.com

Copyright 2017

World War I was fought between the Allied Powers and the Central Powers, which were the two major alliances of countries. In this book, we will be learning about these two different powers.

ALLIED POWERS

The Allied Powers largely formed to defend themselves against the violence of the Central Powers and Germany. They were also referred to as the Entente Powers since they started as an alliance between Britain, France, and Russia known as the Triple Entente.

THE COUNTRIES OF
THE ALLIED POWERS

FRANCE

On August 3, 1914, Germany declared war against France. France was already preparing for war once Germany and Russia went to war. Most of the fighting that occurred along the Western Front was inside of France.

BRITAIN

Once Germany invaded Belgium, Britain decided to enter the war and on August 4, 1914, to declare war on Germany. In order to stop Germany's advance across Western Europe, the British troops joined the French troops.

British World War 1 Soldiers

6й САПЕРН. ЗАПАСН. БАТ.
СПИТЕ БОРЦЫ за СВОБОДУ
СПИТЕ СПОКОЙНОЙ ДУШОЙ
СЧАСТЬЕ ВЫ ДАЛИ НАРОДУ
ВЂЧНАЯ ПАМЯТЬ ВАМЪ
ВЂЧНЫЙ ПОКОЙ!
ПЕТРОГРАДСКІЙ КУРЬЕРЪ
Russian Revolution

RUSSIA

The Russian Empire became an early entry once Germany declared war with them on July 31, 1914. They knew that Russia would protect Serbia from the invasion by Austria-Hungary who was an ally of Germany. Also included in the Russian Empire was Finland and Poland. On March 3, 1918, Russia separated from the Allied Powers after the Russian Revolution, and signed a peace treaty with Germany.

UNITED STATES

The United States had tried remaining neutral, but entered the war on April 6, 1917 as an ally of the Allied Powers and declared war on Germany. The United States mobilized approximately 4,355,000 troops during the war and approximately 116,000 lost their lives.

Russian Revolution

Other countries included with the Allied Powers were Italy, Japan, Brazil, Belgium, Montenegro, Greece, Serbia and Romania.

Georges Clemenceau

FRANCE

GEORGES CLEMENCEAU: From 1917 to 1920 he was Prime Minister of France and he helped in keeping France together during the difficult times. He was given the nickname of "The Tiger". He represented France during the peace talks and advocated for severe punishment for Germany,

King George V

BRITAIN

DAVID LLOYD GEORGE: He was Britain's Prime Minister during most of the war and was an advocate of entering the war and he kept Britain together during this time.

King George V: George V was King of Britain during this time, and even though he had little power, he would often visit the front to inspire their troops.

RUSSIA

TSAR NICOLAS II: As leader of Russia during the beginning of WWI, he entered the war to defend Serbia. Unfortunately, this effort became disastrous to the Russian people. In 1917, the Russian Revolution took place and he was removed from power. In 1918, he was executed.

Nicholas II of Russia

Woodrow Wilson

UNITED STATES

PRESIDENT WOODROW WILSON: After President Wilson was re-elected on his platform for keeping America out of the war, he did not have much choice but to declare war on Germany in 1917. Wilson then advocated for less harsh terms on Germany after the war, realizing that if Germany had a healthy economy it would be of great importance to all of Europe.

MILITARY COMMANDERS OF THE ALLIED POWERS

- France: Marshall Ferdinand Foch, Robert Nivelle, Joseph Joffre
- Britain: Douglas Haig, Herbert Kitchener, John Jellicoe
- Russia: Aleksey Brusilov, Nikolai Ivanov, Alexander Samsonov
- United States: General John Pershing

General Ferdinand Foch

World War I

CENTRAL POWERS

The Central Powers started as an alliance between Austria-Hungary and Germany. The Ottoman and Bulgaria later became a part of the Central Powers.

THE COUNTRIES OF THE CENTRAL POWERS

GERMANY

Germany was the prime leader of the Central Powers, having the largest army. Its strategy at the beginning of the war was referred to as the Schlieffen Plan, which demanded a quick takeover of France as well as Western Europe. Germany could then concentrate on Russia and Eastern Europe.

German Soldier

AUSTRIA-HUNGARY

The assassination of Archduke Ferdinand was essentially the beginning of World War I. Austria-Hungary believed that Serbia was responsible for the assassination and proceeded to invade Serbia, which set off the events that resulted in the war.

OTTOMAN EMPIRE

With strong economic ties with Germany, The Ottoman Empire signed an alliance with them in 1914. Eventually, the entrance into war led to the downfall of the Empire and the formation of a country known as Turkey in 1923.

Western Front Battleground

BULGARIA

Bulgaria become the last major country joining with the Central Powers in 1915. They claimed land that Serbia held and they were eager to invade Serbia.

THE CENTRAL POWER LEADERS

GERMANY

Kaiser Wilhelm II: He was the last Kaiser (also referred to as Emperor) of the German Empire and was related to George V, the King of England and the Tsar of Russia. His policies became the reason for the war. Eventually, he lost the army's support and had little power by the end of this war. In 1918, he abdicated the throne and left the country.

Kaiser Wilhelm II

Emperor Franz Josef

AUSTRIA-HUNGARY

Emperor Franz Josef: For 68 years, Josef was the ruler of the Austrian Empire. With the assassination of Archduke Ferdinand, he proceeded to declare war with Serbia which was the start of World War I. Josef died in 1916 during the war and Charles I was his successor.

OTTOMAN EMPIRE

Mehmed V: During World War I, he was Sultan of the Ottoman Empire and in 1914 declared war on the Allies. In 1918, he died right before it ended.

Sultan Mehmed V

Ferdinand I of Bulgaria

BULGARIA

Ferdinand I: During WWI, he was the Tsar of Bulgaria. At the end of the war, he gave up the throne to his son, Boris III.

THE CENTRAL POWERS MILITARY COMMANDERS

- Germany - General Franz Conrad von Hotzendorf, Field Marshal Paul von Hindenburg, General Erich von Falkenhayn, Helmuth von Moltke, Erich Ludendorff
- Austria-Hungary - Archduke Friedrich
- Ottoman Empire - Enver Pasha, Mustafa Kemal

Franz Conrad von Hötzendorf

WHERE DID MOST OF THE FIGHTING TAKE PLACE?

Most fighting occurred in Europe along the eastern front and the western front. The western front consisted of a line of trenches from Belgium all the way to Switzerland. Most of it that took place along this front occurred in Belgium and France. The eastern front consisted of Germany, Bulgaria, and Austria-Hungary on the one side, and Romania and Russia on the other side.

Battle of the Marne

THE MAJOR BATTLES

Most of the war was fought along the western front using trench warfare. The soldiers barely moved at all and just shot and bombed each other from the trenches across from each other. Some of the major battles included the First Battle of the Marne, the Battle of Tannenberg, the Battle of the Somme, the Battle of Verdun and the Battle of Gallipoli.

TRENCH WARFARE

Trench warfare is a form of fighting that takes place when both sides construct deep trenches to protect themselves against their enemy. They can stretch for several miles and can make it almost impossible for advancement by either side. The western front was fought during WWI using trench warfare and towards the end of 1914, both sides had created trenches that spanned from the North Sea, through Belgium, as well as France. Neither side, as a result, gained much ground during the three-and-a-half-year time period from October of 1914 to March 1918.

Western Front

World War 1 Trench

CONDITIONS WITHIN THE TRENCHES

They were far from being clean, nice places, and actually they were quite disgusting. They would contain all types of different pests living within the trenches that included lice, frogs and rats. Rats were found all over and would get into their food and eat about everything, including soldiers that were sleeping. Lice also became a big problem, making the soldiers itch terribly and resulted in a disease referred to as Trench Fever.

Weather conditions also added to the rough conditions found in the trenches. Rain would cause flooding in the trenches and they would get muddy and flood. The mud would clog their weapons and make it difficult to move for battle. The consistent moisture might also cause the infection that became known as Trench Foot, which, if not treated, could get so bad they would have to amputate a soldier's foot. Cold weather would be dangerous as well and soldiers would often lose fingers or toes due to frostbite and some even died from exposure to the cold weather.

Trenches of the battlefield at Vimy France

Galerie des Glaces

HOW DID WORLD WAR I END?

On November 11, 1918, the fighting ended once a general armistice was agreed upon by both sides. The signing of the Treaty of Versailles was the official end of the war between Germany and the Allies.

CASUALTIES

The Allied mobilized approximately 42 million military personnel during this war. Approximately 12,925,000 were wounded in action and about 5,541,000 were killed. The two countries with the most number of soldiers killed during the war were France with about 1,400,000 and Russia with about 1,800,000.

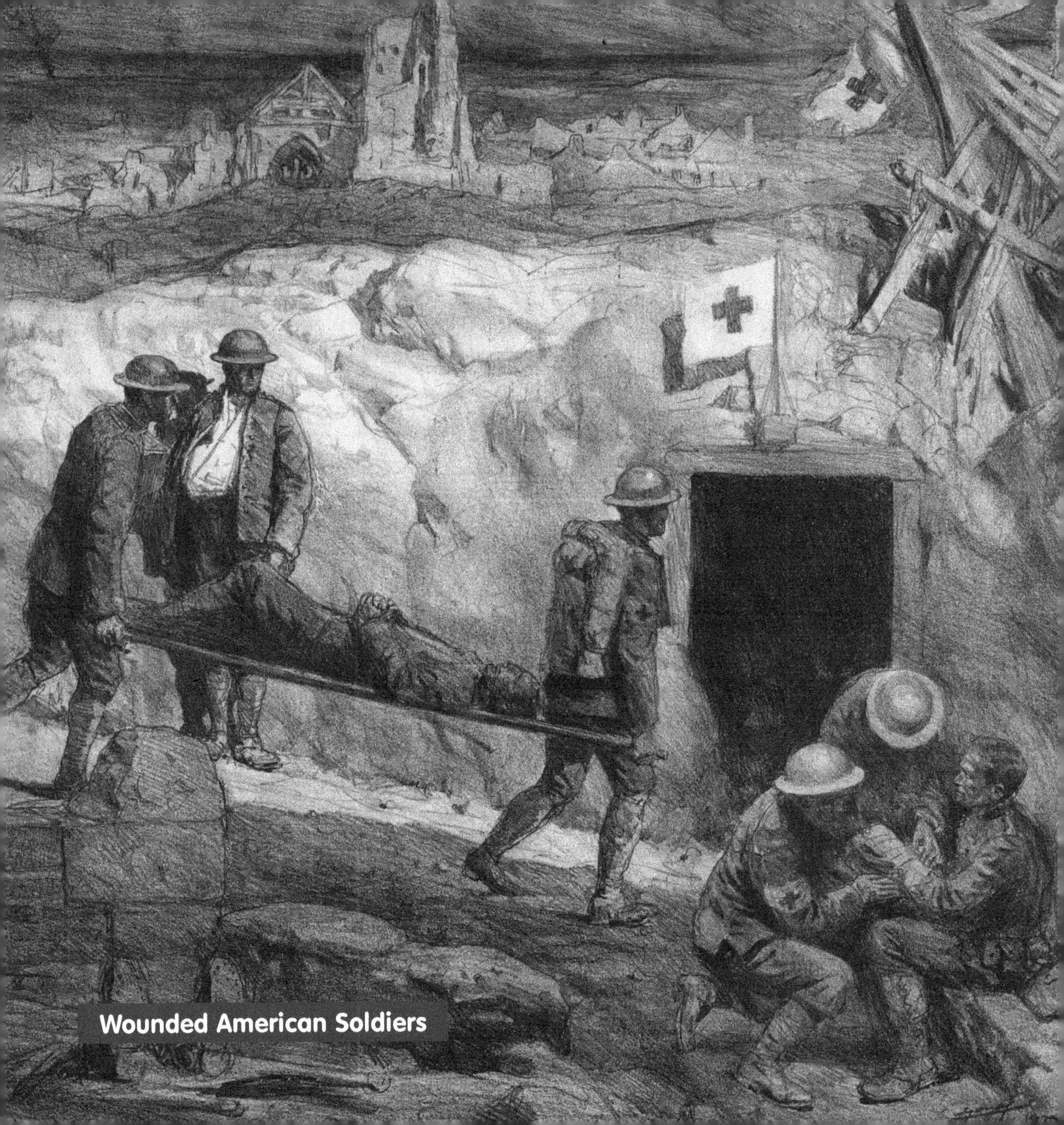

Wounded American Soldiers

World War I was a major conflict fought between 1914 and 1918.
Other names for World War I include the First World War, WWI,
the War to End All Wars and the Great War.

For additional information about World War I and the Allied and Central Powers, you can go to your local library, research the internet, and ask questions of your teachers, family and friends.

Visit

BABY PROFESSOR
EDUCATION KIDS

www.BabyProfessorBooks.com

to download Free Baby Professor eBooks and view
our catalog of new and exciting Children's Books